ANNIE M HENDERSON

Later in Life Lesbian

*Coming Out Later in Life & Leaving Fear,
Overwhelm, & Guilt Behind*

Contents

1

Introduction

Βut...but, I did everything I was supposed to do. I checked off all the boxes for a "successful" life.

Married... Check!
Bachelor's degree...Check!
Master's degree...Check!
Career...Check!
Build a house... Check!
Have a healthy baby...Check!
Go to church...Check!

"...I don't understand. I have it all. We don't fight. He doesn't abuse me in any way.

He's a good guy.

So why do I feel so stuck?

Why don't I feel truly happy deep down?

Why does it feel like something is missing when I've done everything "right"?

This was 15 years ago.

This book isn't meant to have all the answers or even be a quick fix. When I was having what I now call my "Awakening", I would have given anything to have had a book like Untamed by Glennon Doyle or anything else that could have helped me not feel so alone and broken. This small book is an attempt to help fill that gap. To inspire and give hope, no matter where in the world you are reading or listening to this.

Now, as a Life Coach, it is my life's purpose to help women struggling with the same fear, doubt, guilt and confusion to know that they are not alone and that nothing is wrong with them. They are not bad or damaged and they have always been enough.

Hear me when I say, I see you. You are whole and worthy of the life that awaits you. By hearing my journey, my purpose for this book is to bring you hope.

"A lot of times people coming out later in life have been people pleasers since they were little. They were domesticated from a young age. Taught how to act. What's okay and what's not okay. And they get to a point in their life where they realize they're just not happy...
Instead of a midlife crisis, it's an awakening. A rebirth that should be celebrated because this is who they really are."

Annie M Henderson

2

Growing Up People-Pleasing in Texas

U nlike my partner who knew at the age of 5 that she was gay, my process took a lot longer. I believe this may have something to do with a mixture of internalized homophobia and the term my own child taught me, demisexual. Don't you just love the fact that we can learn from a child just as much as we can from someone with their doctorate?

"Demisexuality is a sexual orientation characterized by only experiencing sexual attraction after making a strong emotional connection with a specific person. A demisexual identity is a useful indicator for where a person might fall on the asexual spectrum." (dictionary.com)

Although I realized labels can be helpful and broaden our vocabulary, sometimes they can be used to put us right back into a box. We should use them as a tool, not something to further confuse ourselves.

Keep reading to the end for a humorous story when I was first meeting my parter and how being a demisexual comes into play. It is pretty funny now, but was confusing and even a little frustrating back when it happened.

But first, the beginning:

I was raised Catholic in a small Texas town.

I remember my family going to confession and my oldest brother sharing one of his "sins" to confess afterward. I couldn't think of many so I borrowed one of his. I was already trying so hard to do it right...by doing it wrong.

This pattern turned out to be most of my young adulthood and throughout my twenties. It wasn't until decades later that I realized I was a massive people-pleaser. If you follow me online, you are VERY familiar with this term. Let's quickly go over some of the traits of people-pleasers:

- *Usually there is low self-worth.*
- *Goes with the flow.*
- *Struggles to say no (without guilt).*
- *Avoids conflict and tough conversations.*
- *Often apologies even when they aren't to blame.*
- *Constantly feeling exhausted and overwhelmed.*
- *Typically puts others first and takes things personally.*

I could go on, but are some of these starting to sound like you (or someone you love)?

Even though I work with my clients on people-pleasing and help them to finally get to be their authentic selves, this book is about how it showed up in my life and held me back in different ways.

4

Growing up in Texas, I had loads of Southern Baptist friends that I hung out with to participate in choir and do fun youth activities. The feeling of being broken and needing to be fixed and saved arises when I think of the altar calls, loud music, and tears flowing in the crowded gym. Technically, how many times and how many denominations did I need to not go to hell? The fear was real…

In a small Texas town in the 80s and 90s, there was zero representation when it came to the LGBTQIA+ community. What I knew about being gay I learned from churches and talk show hosts with screaming and gasping audiences during the summers, and as you can guess, it wasn't positive.

Unfortunately for those of you like my partner, you heard at an early age words like "abomination" and applied it to yourself, determined to tell no one.

I, on the other hand, was, in my own words, clueless. My days were filled with music lessons and playing every sport my parents would let me. In my smaller town back in the 80s, I played on the "boys" teams for soccer, basketball, baseball, and eventually played volleyball, soccer, and softball in highschool. I didn't recognize my attraction for anyone. Here is where the people-pleasing came in… if a guy asked me out, I said yes. Less of dating and more of an instant boyfriend. When I would break it off, the next guy would come along to ask me out. As someone that doesn't dance, I went to all of my boyfriends' dances and multiple proms. Like most people-pleasers, I was very agreeable. On the surface, agreeableness seems like a nice thing. What I noticed with myself and clients is that it usually meant not truly knowing who you are and what you like. Sound familiar?

I met my ex husband at the age of 17, ironically enough, playing softball. He was just finishing up college and at the time this didn't seem like an issue to me. As a mom now, I would have some concerns and conversations. We got engaged and married into a Pentecostal church when I was 19. My mom was definitely not pleased, but she hadn't been happy for a while and we didn't have a close relationship. Granted, this was in my highschool years when my brothers left for college, my dad had some undiagnosed mental illness combined with a traumatic brain injury, divorce, and menopause.

For those of you that are fearful of divorce and what it might do to your children, I was one that was ready for the divorce because of the fighting. As an adult now who has been through divorce and raised a child, I realize there are things about my parents and their relationship that I will never know. I'm sure they tried to fix things from their childhood and make it better for us, just like I did for my kiddo. Hopefully, my child will do the same and so on. The goal for us all is to break the generational curses. It takes awareness and intention to make this happen.

Once I was finally married, I prided myself on our lack of fighting... not realizing that it was a sign of something else. I thought, oh this is fantastic, I've got it all. The white picket fence, as a client likes to say, and no fighting besides some minor critiquing of how I folded his shirts. Mistakenly, I thought I had hit the jackpot. I had checked all the boxes of what I had assumed paved the path to success. Sex was just something I had to do as a married person and judging by my conversations with a couple of other women, it just wasn't that great and a part of marriage... and that was life.

Yikes. I didn't know what was missing, but 70 more years of this didn't sound like a fairy tale.

3

The Catalyst

We were married 6 years before my catalyst entered my life. She was a coworker, and in true demisexual fashion, we were just friends and I was still clueless. I enjoyed spending time with her at work, meeting up to play tennis, and they even had me and my husband over one evening. Believing I had a new best friend that got me was such a fun experience for someone who identified as an introvert at the time and didn't go out much.

Things escalated when out of nowhere, at least in my mind, she shared that she had feelings for me. Even though I hadn't gone there in my mind, as soon as I read those words there was an almost instant realization that THIS is what this was. I had been so oblivious and now so many feelings hit me at once.

Exhilaration!
Confusion!
Fear!
Regret!
Hopeful!

Loss!

…and of course **shame** and *guilt*.

I learned so much about myself in that second that explained so many things. But…but…but I was married and she was married and this could NEVER move forward.

Eternity felt wrapped up into those fleeting seconds, but I'm pretty sure I responded with a rushed, "I feel the same."

I felt safe sharing those words knowing it was impossible to move forward and that we would be on the same page…ya know, because we were married.

Where I assumed we were at a standstill and would carry on as friends, it was like a green racing flag to her meaning, GAME ON!

What had I done…

There was so much texting and chatting. Let me date myself a bit by saying this was in the days before unlimited data and each text cost something and it added up quickly. Imagine your spouse asking about why the bill was so high that month. It was a blood draining question that spiked fear and causes you to automatically hold your breath…

As someone who does value some of what the book on love languages has to offer, I know that my top two are words of affirmation and physical touch. Even though I was getting a version of these at home, it just wasn't the same. It was like there was a missing piece, something deeper that was being filled for the first time ever. A spark. An awakening that I never knew existed. That I didn't even realize was supposed to be there.

Wow.

I had forever been changed. Even though I wasn't technically out of the closet, there was now a part of me that could never be shoved back in no matter how hard I tried or how much fear I had.

It was like being in water with two oars and rowing them in opposite directions. It started out as a constant battle within. Knowing one thing from childhood, the rights and wrongs of life, and KNOWING this part of me that had been covered up, hidden away… lost and silenced.

In the television series, Grey's Anatomy, two female characters, one with experience and one without, are smiling after a night of intimacy. As the experienced one gets up to dress and leave, the other starts laughing and compares the experience to when she first got glasses as a child. She recalls not even realizing she needed the glasses but once she got them…the whole world was different. Magical. Beautiful. New.

Even with this epiphany, there were many nights of tears, prayers, horrible self-talk, and confusion. A feeling of being stuck.

Like many of my clients, I was married to a "good guy." He didn't abuse me in any way, cheat on me, and was an attentive father. Many of us grew up in a time where "stay together for the kids" and "put everyone first" was the battle cry. Why would I give up allllll that I have and start over when things are so safe and consistent right now? Besides, from the outside everything looks picture perfect…

A tug of war between the little devil and angel on my shoulder. The devil shouting words of guilt and "shoulds" and the angel gently offering up love, peace, and freedom.

If you are reading this, you probably know full well which voice was louder. The domesticated, shameful default record that we have been playing on loop for decades.

I want to pause for a moment to discuss our ego and gut and how it plays a role in people-pleasing and oftentimes, staying stuck. When I think of my gut, I like to simplify it as love. Our mind/ego as fear. When that still small voice is sure and confident, it is clear. On the other hand, our ego can be talkative with all the fears and negative what ifs that will come up. For example, "What if I lose everything and everyone?" is a fearful thought from our ego. Our gut is often just a simple "yes", "no", "ugh", or "mmmm!"

People-pleasers tend to not trust themselves. They are used to doing what others want them to do, following rules, and putting on a mask for whoever they are around. We learn to ignore our gut and instead anticipate what others might want and do our best at complying and being agreeable.

This rarely works out for us. Exhaustion and overwhelm kick in because this denial of self is not sustainable.

I was a people-pleaser since around middle school.
    As I mentioned, people-pleasing tendencies usually include:

- *Difficulty saying "no" to others.*
- *Guilt when they do say no.*
- *Resentment from saying yes.*

- *Over apologizing, even when they weren't responsible.*
- *Avoiding conflict/difficult conversations.*
- *Taking things personally.*
- *Putting self last and running on fumes.*

4

Religion and Shame

Let's talk a bit about religion. As I mentioned before, I was raised Catholic, married into a Pentecostal church, grew up in Texas with no representation and it was just ingrained and taught that if you are gay that you are an abomination and would go to hell. I never heard this growing up in church, but it seemed to be something that was understood.

I remember praying to God to strike me down if this was wrong. There was so much guilt, confusion and I just felt torn and lost. Instead of spiraling further down or being struck down on the spot, I began to feel so peaceful. A realization that God doesn't make mistakes. God created me this way on purpose and it was time to stop hiding away my gifts and myself. It would do no one any good to pretend and lie my way through life just to make others happy.

Fast forward to when Sam and I were looking for a church while living in Sherman, Tx. She even called around and couldn't find anything accepting or anyone willing to say that our family could come there without changing who we are.

We drove to several amazing churches in Dallas but it was just not sustainable to drive that far every week.

Here comes the power of sharing with others when you have a good thing:

Sam's college roommate, who happened to live quite close to me in Sherman also, invited us to their Methodist Church and said there was another gay couple or two and we should check it out. Cue the Heavens shining down upon Mosaic, the modern worship service. Everyone was so friendly, the pastors immediately memorized our names and greeted us every time (…but not in a love bombing kind of way).

This was a church we could join, we could sit next to each other and hold hands like every other couple there. We were invited to be part of the hospitality team, serve communion, and even light the candles during Advent. Ya know, very visual ways to serve as opposed to other churches who sometimes are okay with you singing in the choir, collecting your tithes, and that's about it.

One of my amazing pastors and I began a free Facebook group for LGBTQIA and Allies. A place for people around the world, over 1k members, can reach out for support, ask questions, meet others, talk with pastors if they have questions about being a gay christian or about deconstructing old harmful beliefs… and the best part of all? It's drama free! Woohoo!

Oh wait, it gets better: my town started hosting the annual Grayson Pride event and now a group of us set up in the hot Texas sun every year, interact, talk, laugh, and spend a day with all the beautiful people that come out there to celebrate who they are or those that they love. Come visit sometime!

Finally, the board at our church asked if I, Annie Henderson, a life coach that helps all but mostly the LGBTQIA community, would like to use an office at church to be able to see clients or community members in need of someone to speak to.

Can life get any better?!

5

Divorce and Guilt

Even when I eventually got a divorce, there was still that ingrained thought of "stay together for the kids" which is so outdated and oftentimes does more harm than good. I do believe my parents stayed together longer than was healthy, but I know they did it from a good place in their heart. No parent out there wants to hurt their kids. The important differentiation that needs to be made is that there is a clear and big difference between hurting our kids and harming our kids.

During a divorce, is there a grieving process for everyone involved, even the one that started the process? Most definitely. Both spouses can have hurt feelings and dashed expectations or dreams. Kids can be sad as they learn to adjust to the new normal. In laws, friends, and church members might all have some feelings invested in your relationship and how it affects them.

Harm however is usually based on intention. Are you trying to harm your spouse? No. Are you trying to harm your kids? Of course not.

Usually, a divorce that comes from one person realizing they have been shoving down who they are, ends up being something that involves growth for all. Do your children deserve to see their mommy at her happiest? Living life who she really is? I know my child has benefited greatly from seeing my amazing, loving and healthy relationship play out in front of her.

Now did I have a guarantee that things would turn out this way? Did I even know who Sam was when I got divorced? No and no.

But our exes are not meant to be a safety net. They are not comfort zones we get to hang out in until a sure thing comes along. Sometimes a leap of faith is necessary. For those of you who are still struggling with people-pleasing, it can be hard to know what is right, wrong, your idea, and so on. Especially when those around you are piling their own fears and doubts on top of your own.

This is one very important reason why you need to find a support group, either online or in person, where you can practice telling your story, not being afraid or feeling alone as you grow and become reintroduced to yourself. Warning: not all groups are alike. It can be like dating. You must work on boundaries and recognize red flags. Life is 50/50 and there will always be pockets of people that are fearful, negative and still at the beginning of their healing process.

Don't allow one bad or uncomfortable encounter to stall you out or have you running back into the closet.

A heads up: there is something called a "vulnerability hangover." For people-pleasers, when we start to take our mask off for the first time and share bits and pieces of our authentic self with people we are getting to know or sometimes total strangers, many times once you hit that submit button a flood of feelings can suddenly overwhelm you. If you are lucky, it is pride and confidence. Oftentimes, it can be fear, dread and sometimes you might either delete or hide for a while until you recognize the beautiful and amazing reality that...you didn't die! There are comments and some lovely supportive people out there. Rinse and repeat as you grow your confidence and start to uncover and unearth the real you.

6

Fear and Coming Out

For my mom, whether I am going to be close to Kansas, or if I'm at our local Pride event, she always reminds me, "Be safe." Unfortunately, we still live in a time and world where the LGBTQIA community are a minority that are threatened, killed, and bashed daily.

My own experience, even in North Texas, has been one of love, kindness and respect. Even in a small town, I want you to know that you aren't alone. I will admit that Sam and I aren't the biggest with PDA and we both can usually pass as straight.

For those of you that have a lot of fear around coming out, I highly recommend finding a support group either locally or online so that you can intentionally surround yourself with others you can relate to, celebrate, grow, and reach out to when feeling like you are in a bubble and all alone.

I regularly wear rainbow shirts, bracelets, earrings and instead of hearing hate, it is usually someone that speaks up sharing their appreciation for my accessory. I wear them because it makes a difference in at least one person every time I go out and I am proud to be the representation for that person.

7

Parenting

For a long time I worried about my kid having 2 moms and how her friends other kids at school might treat her. By the way, she would quickly correct me with a smirk that she has 3 moms.

The truth is, if I had stayed married to her father, I would have continued to people-please. I would have hidden away a part of myself and lived out my life of living for others and denying myself thinking it would help my daughter.

Instead, getting my divorce was beneficial for everyone. Choosing to do the work on myself, my child was able to have a healthier, happier mom. After meeting Sam and eventually building a house together, she got to witness what a healthy, respectful, and happy relationship looks like.

- *How to set boundaries.*
- *How to have disagreements without yelling.*
- *How to continue to have lives, friends, travel apart from one another.*
- *How to support each other.*

- *How to encourage one another to grow, stretch, and celebrate all along the way.*
- *How to dream big, travel, and not live a life of fear.*

A couple of important things I learned from the incredible book, The Four Agreements, is to not take things personally and not make assumptions. HIGHLY RECOMMENDED! As a parent, being able to decipher your feelings, thoughts, opinions, hopes and dreams from your childs' is crucial. Otherwise, it can lead to a lot of hurt, defensiveness and confusion. This book was also introduced to my kiddo when she was younger. I wish I had access to it and was able to talk about it when I was her age.

"Oh, she's just being a teenage girl." This was something I heard from my ex and I feel like is a common phrase or thought from many parents. Thinking that this is just normal and almost giving up on our responsibilities and what we can do to make these years better for all.

Does it involve intention and work? Yes.
Possibly awkward conversations? Of course.
Will it be worth it? Absolutely!

Stop to think about your own relationship with your parents growing up. Think about if there was anything that could have been done better… and try it! Don't be afraid that you aren't perfect or that you will mess up. Shame has no place in parenting or in raising your child. If you need help, reach out to me or a local professional so that you can be sure to enjoy this precious time together.

When my child came out to me, she had some pride stickers that she chose to wear on her hand for the first several weeks of school. She ended up happily and proudly sharing some with teachers and friends. Instead of fear or a negative reaction, she was met with love and acceptance. I say this often, but I am SO impressed and amazed with this up and coming generation. If we as parents are intentional about not passing on fear and hate, I truly believe they will save this world!

Living authentically, being a healthy role model and ditching the "do as I say not as I do", is a way to help ensure that both you and your children have a shot at a happier life. Don't wait to have important and big conversations. Waiting until they are teenagers is not advised. Start communicating with your children while they are young so that when they leave the nest, they will know how to stand up for themselves, speak up when uncomfortable, and have an opinion of their own. Having an important conversation one time is not enough- we just don't retain that quickly.

Be the parent you wish you had. Start breaking generational curses and let go of old beliefs, old boundary breaking and start helping your child have healthy communication, healthy boundaries, and appreciating them for who they are, not who you or the grandparents want them to be.

8

On the other side…

And then there was Sam…

As terrible as the toxic relationship was, it provided clarity and contrast when I did meet Sam and found out what true, toxic free love looks, sounds, and feels like. If I had to choose 5 adjectives to describe this life we have created it would be love, easy, fun, communication, and peace. (I could go on!)

One of our favorite things to do is to take a walk with our dog, Skeeter, and to share gratitude for what we have and to dream big on what is to come.

If this is your first time hearing me talk about my relationship, you might assume we are in the beginning honeymoon phase… in 2023 we will be celebrating 12 years!

Were there some early bumps to navigate as I was still recovering from being a people-pleaser? Of course!

Old Annie would turtle up and avoid conflict and conversations. I had to learn that it was safe and healthier to share wants, frustrations, fears and slowly take down my wall instead of fortifying it. It took practice, but we ended up building the most solid foundation. I want you to know that this is possible for you, too. But settling isn't the answer. Your brain will convince you that it is safer in your comfort zone.

Comfort zone does not equal healthy, just predictable.

Okay, you've made it almost to the end and to the section about our life. I promised a funny story about when my partner and I first met so I asked her to write out her own version for your reading pleasure. Enjoy:

"A friend decided to play matchmaker. This was back in the day when we didn't have Tender and all that stuff. So she thought we would be a good match. We had never met each other or seen each other and so she sent me a picture of you just to say, "What do you think?" And I saw a picture of you and I was like, "Yeah, she's beautiful. Totally sign me up- yes!" She sent a picture of me to you and you were like "NOOOOOOO, what are you thinking?! I'm not into that." And so, I got rejected."

I hoped you had a good chuckle from that dramatic reenactment! Of course, I didn't say ANY OF THAT, but it still makes me laugh. I actually recorded her telling the story and transcribed it. I had to edit out all the laughter between us.

Here was the ah-ha I had from this experience later on when my child taught me about the word demisexual.

25

I didn't know it at the time, but I am not someone who can just fall in love with a picture or even the first time I meet someone. Even the FABULOUS Cate Blanchett had to win me over throughout several incredible movies and performances. Being demisexual, I need to get to know someone and connect on an emotional level first. Sam obviously, not so much.

The great news, fast forward and we happened to meet at a mutual friend's birthday party and from there I messaged her and then I got my lovely emotional connection that I so desperately craved.

9

Coaching and Ripple Effects

Life Coach - like a personal trainer for your brain.

My word for the year is ripple effects. I wrote the following at the end of 2022 at a coaching event:

> "I will change the lives of people around the world and for generations to come.
> Healthier lives.
> Healthier families.
> Healthier future."

As a life coach, I have the honor of helping support and guide women with struggles similar to what I experienced. I understand the guilt, the people-pleasing and living a life where the focus is on everyone but myself and I'm pleased to be able to provide tools, resources and to be able to hold space as women like you, start to rediscover themselves. Remember, it is never too late to change.

If you or someone you know is interested in trading in negative self-talk and labels that include

- Stuck
- Broken
- Unlovable
- Worthless
- Guilty
- Selfish

…for a more empowering way to view ourselves and our life that sounds a little more like:

- Love
- Peace
- Confident
- Happy
- Fulfilled
- Inspired
- Empowered
- Free

Then please reach out by going to my website *anniemhenderson.com* for a free consultation call.

I 1000% love what I do, who I help, the lives I affect and the generations that are impacted. To be able to help one person who then makes healthier decisions, breaks generational curses, and changes the mindset of those around them, both at home and work, by living their authentic lives….it doesn't get much more beautiful than that.

My wish is that my own journey can give inspiration and hope as you navigate your own.

About the Author

Annie M Henderson is a Certified Professional Life Coach specializing as a Coming Out Coach for the LGBTQIA community and helps people-pleasers that avoid conflict, over apologize, and struggle to say no, start living authentically and find the peace they have been missing.

After going from an unfulfilled existence checking all the boxes of perceived "success," to breaking into an intentional, abundant life, she now uses her experiences and professional background as a teacher, counselor, and life coach, to teach and mentor others. In working with her diverse clientele to discover unapologetic joy, including the LGBTQIA community and people-pleasers, her teachings focus on releasing self-doubt, embracing the power in setting boundaries, and removing the habit of over apologizing. She's the international best-selling co-author of She Did It!, which follows women from around the world and their transformational journey.

Annie's masters degrees in education, school counseling and professional counseling, complement her mission and inform her regular content shared with loyal followers on TikTok and Facebook. Annie's insights have been featured in Open Mike Podcast, VeryWellMind, Medium, and The Jeff Crilley Show.

You can connect with me on:

🌐 https://www.anniemhenderson.com
📘 https://www.facebook.com/anniemhenderson
🔗 https://www.tiktok.com/@anniemhenderson

Printed in Great Britain
by Amazon

37193557R00030